POETIC SYMBIOSIS

Poetic Symbiosis

Surviving Addiction and Mental Illness

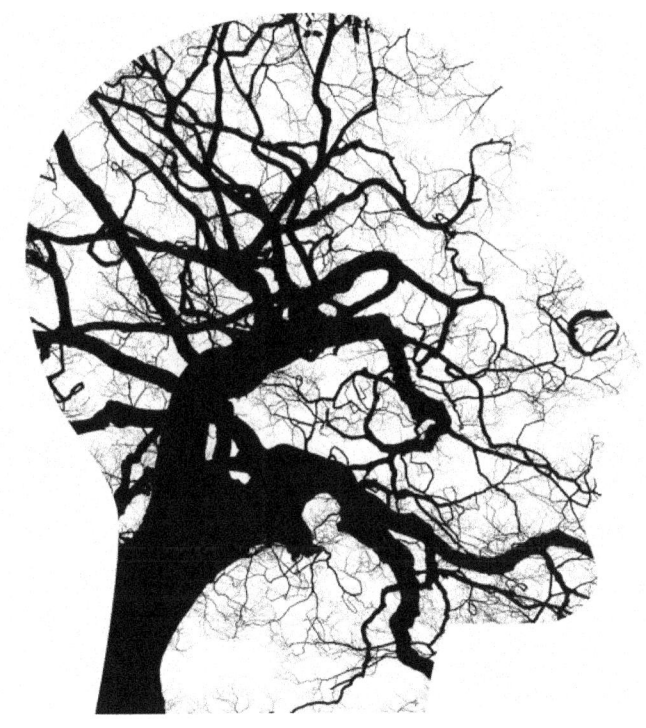

Matt Loat and Docrobin

This edition published 2020 by:
Takahe Publishing Ltd.
Registered Office:
77 Earlsdon Street, Coventry CV5 6EL

Copyright © Matt Loat and Docrobin 2020

ISBN 978-1-908837-15-8

The moral rights of the authors have been asserted.

All rights reserved. This publication may not be reproduced, stored in a retrieval system or transmitted, in any form or by any means, electronic, mechanical, photocopying, recording or otherwise, without the prior permission of the publishers.

Internal images courtesy of Pixabay
Front cover image courtesy of art-now-and-then
Back cover image courtesy of Travis Rupert from Pexels

TAKAHE PUBLISHING LTD.

2020

To the memory of Mark Vincent Loat and Allan Peter Toft,
the loss of whom had a profound effect on their families

Acknowledgements

We would like to thank the following for their support, understanding and friendship:

Yvonne, Samantha, Amber, Duncan, Diane, Lee, Fern, Harvey, Leo, Russell, Chris, Mikayla, Shannan, Jenna, Emily S, Benjamin, Mary, Anita, Hazel, Adrian, Sarah, Benita, Mark W, Terry, Agro, Mark L, Madison, Noah, KT, Harper, Kam, Ian, Simon M, Becky T, Russell J, Simon P, Kam S, Patricia C, Bob R, Ian F, Carole D, Indy T, Marie M, Prince M, Emily T, Rednits, Anne B

CONTENTS

Introduction	1

Part 1: Who's Who?

Addictshead Revisited	4
Voices	5
A Camera for a Day	6
Hopeless?	8
Rubik's Cube of Narcotics	10
Hope	11
A Stereotype?	12
DecideErrata	13
My Heroine in Heroin	14
Mon Frère Cauchemardesque	16
Shut That Door	18
Why So Serious?	19
Are You Happy?	20
Boundaries Unbound	21
Changing Life	22
Dead to the Family	23
Getting Better	24
Have You Ever?	25
I Woke Up Today	26
Why?	26
Waterloo	26
I'm a Ghost	27

My Invisible Illness	27
OK	28
Last Text	28
School of Life	29
Miranda Rights	30
Shadows and Dust	32
Stronger Together	33
That Devil	34
The Tunnel	35
The Light of Recovery	36
The Ward	38
The Drug Dealer	40
Today	41

Part 2: This is Us

An Eternal Labyrinth	44
Death of a Dream	46
Containing Chaos	47
Forgiveness?	48
Sent to Coventry	49
Mélangé dans l'unité	50
Therapy Unmasked	51
Lapine Lore	52
La Guerre Cérébrale	53
Will Power or Willpower?	54
De-Termination	56
E Pluribus Unum	57

Final Dilemma	58
Labelling Faux Pas	59
Constructive Distraction	60
Perfidious Faith	61
Liquiphrenic Conversation?	62
Guerrilla Warfare	63
Multimasking	64
Mechanically Human	65
Crisis of a Human Rose	66
Not Like That	68
Doolally in Deolali	70
La Bête Noire	72
Eternal Labyrinth II	74
The Addiction Clover	75
The A to Z of Mental Health and Addiction	76
The Z to A of Recovery	77
Trigger Happy	78
Sobriety Junktion	79
Intro & Cockney on the Cobbles	80

Epilogue

Isolate and Collaborate: Antithesis?	82

Introduction

Matt and the Doc are decades apart in age and an unlikely partnership in poetry, one with a troubled education and the other a postdoctoral university graduate. One with mental health issues of flexible diagnosis and the other an alcoholic in recovery. Meeting by chance through a mix of social and family connections they discovered that they have a shared interest in using poetry as a therapeutic tool. Each having written numerous poems individually and having discussed their respective issues and management, they were astounded at the remarkable parallels between mental health and addiction in their broadest senses. Both have had experience in supporting others plagued by addiction, whether it be through alcohol or drugs, and some form of cooperation seemed inevitable

After very brief discussions outside a local supermarket, the decision was made that they would collaborate in a series of poems bringing these unlikely mental health siblings together. One of the common things that these issues share is the value of talking or writing about personal experiences, both as a purgative process and realisation for the individual that they are not alone in their situation. Shared experience is so valuable in these areas and can give hope to those who appear to be doing less well.

This collection has been arranged into two sections. The first is a selection of poems from each side of the coin, hoping to illustrate their similarities. We leave it up to you to decide who's who! The second is the result of their collaboration to date, representing a blend of their personal experiences.

Hopefully you will find their efforts both interesting and supportive. I have known these two reprobates for several years and they do represent success in their respective battles.

Mary Fingal, 2020

Poetic Symbiosis

Poetic Symbiosis

Part 1: Who's Who?

Both of us are a bit crazy, but who is responsible for each poem?

Are they in any particular sequence?

You decide!

Poetic Symbiosis

Addictshead Revisited

I am your addiction, I am your disease
More cunning than cancer, not treated with ease
Keep ignoring me, that suits me just fine
Do so much longer and I'll make you whine

A real double agent you thought was your friend
Now that I have you prepare for your end
Lying-in-wait your backside to bite
You try to suppress me, one hell of a fight

Use your 12 Steps or psychological tools
Either way, you are nothing but fools
I will get you if you drop your guard
It's my job to make it that hard

Recovery's a noun that comes from a verb
With a past tense, in grammatical blurb
Sadly for you, in my case there's none
You fight me forever, or else I have won

Part 1: Who's Who?

Voices

That exocet is truly a modern day Robin Hood
You've stolen my sanity I'm evil beyond bad or good
Those explosive rants like volcanic dragon's fire
Please stop I'm sorry I'm broken and tired

Like the hurricanes my mind is in a maelstrom
Can't stop my body isn't in control what's done is done
Blood soaked fists and tears like acid waterfalled on my cheeks
I'm sorry my masters your servant is lowly and weak

Your wish is my command let me be your genie
Not aboded in a lamp but in my whole vicinity
Aladdin's thievery is not a skill I desire or crave
I'm the real wonder of the world much more than a cave

Do you hear my voice on the wind, my precious I'm talking?
Not talking to you but three heads are better than one my King
This internal conversation this damn hydra effect
If only our hamadryad her fangs their toxicity delicious I bet

The trials of a demigod and failures of a trinity
That Polynesian decapod was right it's better to be shiny
Three strikes and you're out guillotined and quart
I never signed a contract this trio has no accord

The chocolate mountain with the silver T is for us all
I will have resurrection from these demon depths to which I fall
In life you can only let it go control change and have choice
It's not which one is loudest but listen to your truest voice

Poetic Symbiosis

A Camera for a Day

They say the eyes are the gateway to the soul
To me the eyes are high focused cameras
Capturing millions of priceless images
To be stored in the album of the brain.

From snowflakes of delicate lace and crystal feel
The thrashing of the oceans upon soft golden sand,
Those very sands where we leave the gift of footprints
To show the journey we've walked.

In the coldest winds and hottest suns
Springs fresh with morning dew
To autumn evenings abreast a stoked camp fire
With lyrics from the stars and the melody of the moon

That shines like a celestial compass
Through the purple labyrinth in the skies.
The beauty of all animals that walk aside us in this path
To the vol de mort of the loneliness that nips us from the shadows

A recording that we can never stop
The longevity of the tape that never runs out
A soundtrack stuck on repeat
A chorus that we know only too well

The words cannot be seen or changed.
Naked as each dawn brings a new chapter
Of a book that cannot be completed
An exodus with no ending.

The calmness of folded shutters
Can't hide the pictures in the dark
Not battery operated but internal
The human Nikon runs on human heart.

Part 1: Who's Who?

You can't stop time with every spin
The dual arrows on the englassed face
That compass only shows in broken pictures
The motion of our lives can never be replaced

Poetic Symbiosis

Hopeless?

It started with a spliff
Should've thought then – what if
If only you'd listened
To one more wizened

Chilled and relaxed, not angry
Having a laugh, feeling hungry
Those were the days my friend
You thought they'd never end

Weed, grass, puff, blow
How on earth could you know
There isn't a safe way
This was your gateway

Onwards and downwards, the path that you chose
Uppers, downers, sleepers, trippers, all of those
A terrible slide, nowhere to hide
Might have been better if you had died?

Crackhead, smackhead, liar and thief
Couldn't afford to buy any beef
Swallow, smoke, snort, or inject
Not knowing what to expect

Could be an overdose, maybe not
Bacteria and viruses you had forgot
You got an infection because of injection
What did you face then – rejection?

That, the least of my worries
As death rapidly approaches
Sickness and disability on the way down
Makes me do more than just frown

Part 1: Who's Who?

If only you'd listened
To one more wizened
Wouldn't be so frightened
You'd have been enlightened

Poetic Symbiosis

Rubik's Cube of Narcotics

The demon drink
My brethren's curse
Our devil's advocate serpentine
Its venom the darkness gives birth

Toxic is the tonic of candy for the nose
Poppies in the veins with chasing dragons
And rainbows of ecstasy polluting our brains

A habit to be social a broken network
Of choice the prediction of addiction
Is a lonely road of loss and sorrow

Awaken in that den for no promise of tomorrow
Bottom of the barrel
The casks ran dry
Question is the low really worth the high?

Part 1: Who's Who?

Hope

Abandon all hope ye who enter here
So says the sign at the place they sell beer
Not knowing the meaning
I went in there beaming

It took many years before it got a hold
Each one of them increasingly bold
Every time I thought I could cope
Till at last I lost all hope

Two bouts at rehab to unburden my soul
Meeting after meeting I dug a deep hole
Spiral into chaos lasting five years
Helpless and homeless it ended in tears

Losing everything there was no return
Only one outcome - in hell I would burn
In the bleakest, darkest depression
Much too late for further confession

But hope springs eternal in the human breast
In depths infernal you can still give your best
There is help out there from people who care
You've just got to find them somehow, somewhere

For me they worked wonders
Without any blunders
Helping find that strength from within
They gave me the willpower not to give in

Poetic Symbiosis

A Stereotype?

I guess we've all seen him
A young lad, tall and slim
Looking quite shifty outside the shops
He's just checking there aren't any cops

A hand in his pocket, whips out his phone
A glance at the screen, still all alone
Glancing to the left then to the right
The one he's expecting not yet in sight

More glances at the phone, pacing around
Looking quite nervous, not making a sound
Now pacing much further, back and forth
Spotting his mate, just heading north

They pass in the street, a brief touch of fingers
Just saying hello, neither one lingers
All that stress, oh what a drag
A great deal of effort to get a small bag

Part 1: Who's Who?

DecideErrata*

Go placidly amid the noise and haste. Remember to absorb all the negativity. As far as possible, without surrender, take them for all you can get. Speak gibberish loudly and aggressively to those who try to ignore you. Avoid doctors and counsellors, they may actually try to help you.

Compare yourself with others; you are far superior to mere mortals who do not understand. Enjoy your highs for they will not last long before you are in the pits of despair once more. Keep an interest in all substances for there are always new ones to try. Exercise caution in your conversations for the world is full of undercover cops. But let not this blind you to the inevitability of your actions; many persons have died believing, like you, that they are invincible.

Be someone else. Especially do not admit to your addiction. Neither be positive about recovery, for all it will bring is the health and prosperity you can do without. Ignore the experience of those in recovery for they are dull and boring. Nurture your strength and ability to score again and again; it is not your money you are spending. But do not distress yourself with imagining a life without addiction; do not fear a life of exclusion. Be wholesome in your drive to survive on the streets.

You are a child of the universe, no less than the trees and stars; you have a fundamental right to cause chaos. Whether or not it is clear to you, you will die young. Therefore, be at peace with your demons whatever they are. They will help you to achieve your goal of an early grave. For the rest of us, this dreary sham of a world can be a beautiful place as we try to be cheerful, strive to be happy and live long.

The choice is yours.

*With credit to "Desiderata" by Max Ehrmann, 1927

Poetic Symbiosis

My Heroine in Heroin

It all started with that crisp purple note
Its value a mere twenty pounds to you
Now to me I just brought a piece of paradise
My own ecstasy and utopia, I'll soon be there

As I open that chemist's party bag like a child at Christmas
My palms leak with uncontrollable anticipation
Emancipation from this surrounding darkness
Free from the cold slavery of reality and responsibility

The small spoon and the inviting syringe
Side by side in this heavenly marriage
Brown powder citrus and the passionate flames
Under the bed that intense intercourse

Orgasmic bubbling as the serum ejaculates
Climaxing into a sweet opium liquid
Devoured by the syringe as it gives in to provocation
Finely prepared my pièce de résistance

That belted anaconda hugs my arm tight
Its constriction dominates the serpents in my body
Then that needle's kiss breaks my walls and strokes my vein
Then the back wash of blood mélange with that liquid luck

I press down that magic button the venom injected deep
I'm floating on pillowed clouds adorned with millions of stars
The numbness as I close my eyes that waterfall of tranquillity
Every breath I take tastes like the sweetest candy

Part 1: Who's Who?

I hope this never ends as my personal strawberry sunsets
Lowering its head deep into the embrace of the rainbow
Sudden fireworks exploding like a thunderstorm in a cage
Electricity vibrates through my body catapulting me through that tunnel

Escaping the Nirvana is now behind me
Lights rape my sight as I feel arctic in front a human fire
My senses desert me, cowards or casualties in war
Eyes closed before the abandonment of my conscious

I hear echoes and sounds of some familiarity
Overdose I know that word I've met him once before
White coated angels with compassion and serenity
The ones who became my heroine the ones who saved me

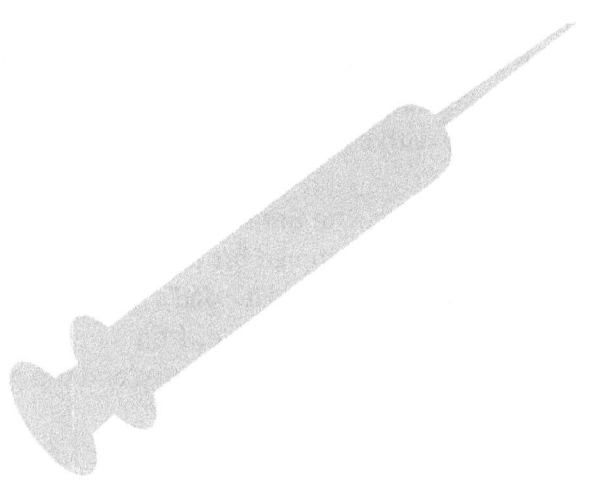

Poetic Symbiosis

Mon Frère Cauchemardesque

Once upon a time there was Mattie and Mark
Two brothers born two years apart
Early memories I have few
Except for the ones that made me hate you

The time you tipped me from my pram
The day that we got Nala, our very first cat
Playing Sega in the corner you always hogged that
Remember when you'd steal my toys and I'd give you a slap

Next few are a bit hazy not everything is clear
Still the times in Nan's caravan I will always treasure
Dear Mum and Dad did their best you know
They didn't have it easy watching us two grow

Dennis did his evil deeds that cunt was proper sleazy
Makins is a special place where the six of us would meet
Wellsborne Market too was fun and the roundabout was a treat
Chips in a tray with curry sauce at the cafe just in town

Remember big brother, The Great Camel Race and Grandad's whitened brow
The Batmobile we called it - dad's old black MG
That car was like a rocket, seconds from nought to sixty
Remember going to the club for bingo and the panto

Old George and his walking stick yet he was full of gusto
Now what happened I've never really understood
We've never spoke about it perhaps it's time we should
I was eight and you were ten you know what you did

Part 1: Who's Who?

Maybe you were confused, after all you were just a kid
Now I'm seeing skateboards and a go kart made of wood
Dad made them for us didn't he, he promised us he could
Gladiators in Birmingham and remember our old forts

If we knew then what we know now perhaps we'd understand our war
Nana is never far from my thoughts and she must be close in yours
Fuck, you shared a birthday the 9th of May of course
The allotment in Terry Road, the incident with the rake
Scrumping apples from the tree that was no mistake

Imagine if we'd paid attention what farmers we could've been
Lots of little memories just like ripples in the streams
But the ones that stand out aren't so nice
In fact they make me scream

Cleethorpes then and pleasure Island that was a wild ride
But we couldn't see the dangers you helped shift the tide
You started being silly and we had to come back home
Fast forward to today and I don't hate you anymore

I still don't know why you did it but your punishment is more
Much more than I can put upon on you of that I am so sure
Now thirty three and thirty one it's been a long time
Don't think I'll ever know but I'll always wonder why

Poetic Symbiosis

Shut That Door

Drink and drugs and fuck it all
So you said before your fall
Hit rock-bottom with a thud
All too often drenched in blood

In that deepest, darkest place
No-one wants to see your face
That substance is your only friend
What a life, there seems no end

Poor me, poor me is your cry
No-one helps, you wonder why
Look in a mirror, then discover
The one to help you to recover

Look beyond and you will see
Others who have broken free
They can help like native guides
All of them escaped their hides

Learned their tricks from the trade
With no intention to upbraid
Listen hard and you will learn
Then in hell you will not burn

More effective than professionals
These can be your daily sessionals
They have all been there before
They can help you shut that door

Part 1: Who's Who?

Why so Serious?

Insanic laughter wild like fires on the ocean
Untamed and out of control,
Blood curdling cackles a screaming banshee
Pierces every audio pocket on the wind.
Freedom is escaping the restrictions of normality
The anarchic structure of chaos leads to victorious rebellion.
A diplomatic delirium of surroundings
In the mighty Davy Jones Locker
Enthorned in psychotic smiles
It's in the weird and plagued disturbed souls we can trust
Embrace the madness....
Why so serious?

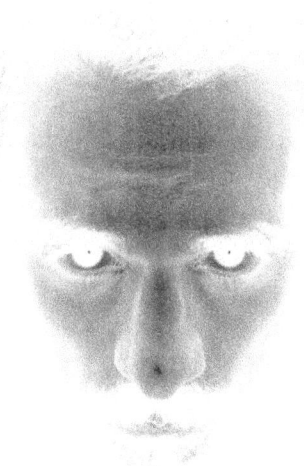

Poetic Symbiosis

Are You Happy?

Are you happy?
When you score that bag
Or swig from the bottle
Chase the winning gamble
Existing only at full throttle

Are you happy?
Running the risk and gambit
Your mind fucked like a jack rabbit
Depression and isolation
Clutching to your vice with chronic desperation

Are you happy?
When your children turn away
Your credit limit breached they demand you pay
In alleys of despair
Or do you simply not care

Are you happy?
The penny drops and you want to quit
They've heard it before and it was bullshit
Questions and doubts you're bombarded with mud
Like a birth you're dressed in blood

Are you happy?
You've been sober and clean for a spell
The people you love listen when you describe hell
You're not the same person you're smiling and dappy
One last time
Are you happy?

Part 1: Who's Who?

Boundaries Unbound

You are immune from mental health and addictions
Then you'd better think again brothers and sisters
These are less predictable than boils and blisters
They may be a surprise with no obvious connections

Not just a condition that may be present from birth
From bad luck, inheritance or a heroin addict mother
They can be lurking in the wings and smiling in mirth
Waiting for that moment when your mind's in a lather

The bite that they give might start with a nibble
Making you notice perhaps with only a dribble
Or they might be savage causing reactions severe
Either way you may have a great deal to fear

With no respect for education, income or social class
The outcomes are predictable, worse than a bite on the ass
Everyone is game in their sinister plot to destroy
It matters not whether you are man, woman, girl or boy

Awareness and recognition are your critical weapons
Giving some ammunition to handle those demons
In addiction you have choice but not always control
With mental health it's just like Calcutta's big black hole

Poetic Symbiosis

Changing Life

Life in recovery is great
That stuff I no longer hate
But treat with respect
And know just what to expect

What is it that changed?
Stopped me being deranged
12 Steps didn't work
I felt such a jerk

Beaten, it was time to give in
That old life went in the bin
Strong coffee and plenty of tea
Loadsa TLC and a soupçon of CBT

Cycle of Change, lapse, relapse and triggers
Tactics and strategies, statistics and figures
People who genuinely cared and openly shared
They were my strength – the ones who had dared

A new understanding of me and that stuff
That's what got me out of the rough
Then strength in unity
That's in the community

A shared common goal
All out of that hole
Helping each other
So we don't smother

With no axes to grind
No miracle to find
Just one desire
Don't re-light that fire!

Part 1: Who's Who?

Dead to the Family

Dead to the family or so it seems
Your favourite pastime shattered their dreams
It always came first
And you did your worst

They tried hard to help you
You persevered too
You just couldn't break it
Then tried to fake it

Finally it broke you
They saw right through you
Finally ejected
Thoroughly dejected

A life all alone
Kicked off your throne
If they don't care
Then hide in your lair

Dead to your family
That's just their homily
Get a grip on reality
In your sobriety

A new life is waiting
It's there for the taking
Hard in the earning
It's what you've been yearning

Poetic Symbiosis

Getting Better

Fear, frustration, isolation, desperation, desolation
We knew the damned lot in our addiction
To hell with them all, we need some hope
Then we can learn how to cope

Not just the immediate strife
With everything the rest of your life
New stuff to learn, a new way of being
New ways of thinking and dealing with feeling

Many ways from which you can choose
A way of your own, so you don't lose
There isn't one right way
It's just like a buffet

Pick and mix the bits that suit best
Anything that stops you 'going west'
Then you'll be clean
A refurbished machine

You'll need regular service
Not just on the surface
It ain't hocus pocus
It needs lots of focus

When you are well
You won't fear that hell
Keep up the good work
And don't be a jerk

Part 1: Who's Who?

Have You Ever?

Have you ever had to watch the ones you love commit suicide
But they don't die they just knock the devil's door
Fixated on the serum of hell they buy
The dependency you have for opioid embers is a chore

"Hey mate it's Ben have you got a dark?"
Hearing your little cousin say that it's a gunshot to the heart,
Begging or blagging with fucking or fighting
The depths to which you've fallen from where I stand are frightening

You're obsessed with those pistons
To your engines you spout excuses not reasons
You hide in the shadows of alleys your cocktail of grog and pills
You think you have immunity but one bad batch kills

Have you ever had to watch them inject that poppy brown?
Just so that they didn't end up cold six feet down
Craving with craziness those withdrawals the pain
You sweat blood with your tears and beg for cocaine

Remember you said "I'm only having the crack"
Well mother fucker you're gonna have a heart attack
The drugs you take damn them they come before everything
That spliff you drag on hell it's destroying your breathing

You idiot you abuse medication yet somehow cheat death,
Whatever you use as your substitute is never enough,
Have you ever watched your loved ones die?
Every time the drugs win they die a little more inside

Poetic Symbiosis

I Woke Up Today

I woke up today
Took my meds and had a shower
Got dressed and looked out the window
Survived the nightmares again
I woke up today

Why?

Why did I wake up this morning?
I've wrecked myself
I've shit the bed
I've fucked it up
I've lost the lot
Why, Oh why, Oh why?
Why did I wake up this morning?

Waterloo

Life's a barrel of shit
At the bottom of the pit
You've never even tried
Might be better if you died
But there is a way out
Have no lingering doubt
The choice yours alone
To try to regain that throne

Part 1: Who's Who?

I'm a Ghost

I'm a ghost
I exist but I'm invisible
You choose not to see me
Yet you can hear my voice
Abandoned
All because of my choice
I'm a ghost
In this world of humanity
You pass and look through me
I'm a ghost
But you CAN see me

My Invisible Illness

My invisible illness
It's real just like me
Because you can't see it
You accuse me dishonestly
My illness is invisible
Yet doubt is in your voice
I never asked for this
My invisible illness
Wasn't my choice

Poetic Symbiosis

OK

I wasn't OK today
That's OK they say
It's OK to not be OK
We can't be OK everyday
So it's OK if I stay away
And it's OK I didn't play
Come what may it'll be OK
Coz it's OK to not be OK

Last Text

As dawn broke on that soft fresh April morning
My world came crashing down like thunder, I'd ignored all the warnings
The cyclone was performing a watery voodoo hex
Then I got the call, tears overflowed as I read your last text

Arrived minutes too late, Mum's Ocean of heartbreak as we embrace
Words will never do it justice what I felt as I saw your face
So peaceful you seemed just like sleeping waiting for that day next
Now I know it's real, the echo of your last text

Ten days of preparation, busied to occupy the pain
Even now the hardest thing, I'll never get to call you Dad again
With Amazing Grace you laid your hat to your one love, you gave it your best
I'll hope to make you proud, I'll carry out that last text.

Part 1: Who's Who?

School of Life

Life is a school
Every road a classroom
Every decision a lesson
New peers we meet
It's a je ne sais quoi
En passant at a bar
Or in line at the shop
Seasons both hot n cold
Graduation or detention
It's very rock and roll
Life is a school
We teach along the way
Ever growing
Not always knowing
Texts of books incomplete
Numbers quite discreet
Professor life the master
Embrace education
Be a student evermore
And absent from detention

Poetic Symbiosis

Miranda Rights

The best way to live in this world is without rules or restrictions
Live life to the fullest let that be your addiction,
Do things on the fly wing it and strive
You think I got a plan hell I just dip duck dodge and dive.

Be fast and furious
No regrets no excuses
Why you so serious
Remember we're born to be free or to raise hell,

We got the moves like Jagger
And street savoir faire
Like Captain Jack be filled with rum and savvy
If you're good at living life never do it for free,

Remember sing it loud and proud
There's things only God can forgive
From the shallow to the deep
You have the greatest show in front of you so swim don't sink,

Takiwatanga in your own time and place
Let's party forever and put a smile on that face
You are not your scars and in the end it really does matter
That we never give up and the glass doesn't shatter,

It's been a long day without our friends
But they live in us till we see them again,
Don't be afraid to exercise Miranda
But Jasmine was right not to be speechless too,

Part 1: Who's Who?

Have desire and drive passion and pride
Please say that under oath
You'll live it to the max with love not loath
It's OK not to be OK and you got a friend in me
So take my hand do you trust let's defy gravity

Poetic Symbiosis

Shadows and Dust

In star-shadowed society we march
Searching for equality
Our individuality is dream cast
Into a world prejudged on fantasy not reality

Mannerisms and blinded responsibility
A nation's children
Plagued by its leaders
Bringing disruptions and toxicity

United are our voices
We stand with dignity
This is our struggle
This is our outcast community

Part 1: Who's Who?

Stronger Together

Why me, oh why, oh why
Our most pitiful and painful cry
With terrible histories
And lives full of miseries

We may ne'er find the answers
On our toes just like ballet dancers
But there is a solution
We can stop that pollution

Make new friends in recovery
What a fantastic discovery
No longer alone
Like dogs sharing a bone

The pack instinct is strong
And it's great to belong
Those longer in the tooth
Sharing their truth

We live and we learn
And when it's our turn
We become a new messenger
Helping aboard the new passenger

A shared wealth of experience
Brings new existence
Just like evolution
Without revolution

Slowly and calmly using both ears
We find that solution that lasts many years
It eases the past and makes a new you
Onwards and upwards the best thing to do

Poetic Symbiosis

That Devil

The past cannot be changed
Not even rearranged
The truth might have hurt
But you've got rid of that dirt

Onwards and upwards is your way now
OK, you might wonder – just how
Just do what you're doing
Stay off the stuff and keep going

In life there is habit
You've broken it, dammit
Now life's a delight
You sleep safe at night

Daytime your life is now bright
And you no longer fight
You've done all your purges
No more surges or urges

You are free from that devil
Your life's on the level
Take one step at a time
Committing no crime

Don't sit on the fence
You know it makes sense
At times there's a trial
Don't slip into denial

Deal with it swiftly
Results can come quickly
Ignore at your own peril
Or again you will see that devil

Part 1: Who's Who?

The Tunnel

That dark tunnel of despair
We have all been right there
Nowhere to turn, nowhere to hide
Terrible thoughts of suicide

Then there's a light at the end
An oncoming train, or a friend?
So hard to tell
It scares you to hell

Only one way to find out
Take a deep breath and reach out
It's one with a lamp
Not just a tramp

He found his way out
And gives you a shout
"Follow me, you can do it
If you can put your mind to it"

Trust one who has been there before
Another has followed, maybe more
Follow him, don't be a dope
Outside there is nothing but hope

An end is in sight
To your terrible plight
There isn't just one way
You'll map your own way

So many directions
You make your selections
Avoiding skins of banana
You can find your nirvana

Poetic Symbiosis

The Light of Recovery

Out of the darkness into the light
It's been such a long hard fight
Ups and downs along the way
Par for the course, so they say

Some find it easier, some find it never
Me in the middle, as ever
No matter, I am here now
Though I do wonder, just how

Solid support from those who've been there
A new set of friends, all of them care
Every one of them solid and sound
I am so glad it was them that I found

They all did it in different ways
Each to their own being the phrase
Together we learn from each other
Our own way we can discover

The peace that it brings I cannot explain
But it has subdued so much inner pain
Life is a joy in its now quiet way
Learning a new way to live, a new way to play

Still have my problems but not every day
Worrying and drinking just doesn't pay
Into the light with a clear head
Has to better than just being dead

Old damage that can't be undone
Doesn't mean life can't be any fun
Just do the right things
See what joy that it brings

Part 1: Who's Who?

The light of recovery shines very bright
Even now I don't get it all right
I just make new mistakes
But keep raising the stakes

Poetic Symbiosis

The Ward

That cold numbness as I walk these halls
Am I the only one to hear them as they call?
Doctors and nurses with their demons and curses
I can't buy my freedom I'm trapped in this asylum hearse

Like a zombie I sit here conscious but withdrawn in this room of pads
They say it's for my own good I'm a danger when I'm mad
Pump you with medications always amending charts and figures
Sectioned for a six to be reviewed in due course it's this that is my triggers

Intense anger Hulk-like as I resist that fucking hug me jacket
Overwhelmed by the force of that needle fresh from its packet
I drop to the sanctuary of the floor I'm safe here right
Couldn't be more wrong the neglect started there that night

Days of an abuse that I can't explain in words
Just look at my arms and chest these cuts fucking hurt
Echoes erupt as they pin me down again
Please someone help me I'm desperate I need a friend

A week or so in I'm not sure I've lost concept of time
They say I'll be here a while it's their way not mine
Quiet tonight the ward seems empty and I really can't cope
The bastard on the inside is right I'll use sheets to make the rope

The noose is ready it fits snug around my throat
I have no final words I have no other way
Too late for regrets I jumped now I'll merely sway
Now they realise that they're murderers with their clipboards and coats

Part 1: Who's Who?

I'm free now and they will live with what they've done
Yes, I needed help but they sent me to a mental prison
Those cunts with their Führer like regimes and dark agenda
Oh what is this place I speak of? Why it's called The Hopeless Centre

Poetic Symbiosis

This Drug Dealer

This drug dealer he is late
He is late again with my eighth
Why do I wait for him he's a waste of time
Oh its coz I need my high

This drug dealer is as punctual as fog
But I'll stay coz I want my grog
Why do I wait for him he's a waste of time
Oh its coz I need my high

This drug dealer has pills and rocks
That time he was early I was really shocked
Why do I wait for him he's a waste of time
Oh its coz I need my high

This drug dealer he's my heroin
When he gives me bags of ketamine
Why do I wait for him he's a waste of time
Oh it's coz I need my high

That drug dealer got tugged by the cops
I'll call the other one when I get to the shops
No longer do I wait for him he's still a waste of time
Waiting for the other one to join me in a line

Part 1: Who's Who?

Today

They used to look down on you
As if you were dog poo
No longer a joke
No more fun to poke

Yesterday remembered with clarity
No more a source of hilarity
Or even disaster
Now your own master

Today is just great
As you lean on the gate
Seeing the world go by
And that lovely blue sky

No looking up from the gutter
Even got bread and butter
The day what you make it
No need to fake it

Tomorrow less certain
Like through a net curtain
A little bit hazy
Definitely not crazy

You learned how to cope
And look forward in hope
To that new day
As good as today

Keep doing the same
No longer a game
Never give in
Don't let it win

Poetic Symbiosis

Poetic Symbiosis

Part 2: This is Us

The following poems are truly united efforts in which we try to explore the sibling relationship between addiction and mental health. They are in the chronological order in which they were written and probably represent the randomly organised nature of our symbiotic thinking. We have found the whole process to be mutually beneficial.

Poetic Symbiosis

An Eternal Labyrinth

Lunatics and addicts all sat in a room
In deep conversation of both wisdom and gloom.
One self-appointed wise man the others all fools
Looks nothing more than a meeting of ghouls

Like a comic book story the meeting begins
Starts with hello then sharing of sins
Dry tears form and evaporate in many an eye
Misplaced narcissistic reminiscing of days gone by

A chorus of thank you and a speaker takes the circle
Is this an address or just another fable?
He preaches about steps – 12 to be precise
Then of a higher power – empty advice

The reality of dependency can only be taught
By those who have lived it in a life that's been fraught
Not stuff from a textbook read by a twit
Just condescending, more like a hypocrite.

Lunatics and addicts, society's down and outs
Abandoned by the system and all with their doubts
They have lived the mysteries of their condition
Finding their own ways, they deserve recognition

Recovery is lifelong with no scripted end
Learn from each other or go round the bend
Much of it might seem off the cuff
But, then, do you want it enough?

Addict or lunatic don't be heartbroken
Though trapped in that tunnel you can be awoken
Not the same as yesterday nor as tomorrow
Understand the despair that filled you with sorrow

Part 2: This is Us

You may think your life is boring and humdrum
There are lessons in this apparent conundrum
Of addicts and lunatics and of their misery
Those you will find throughout your recovery

Poetic Symbiosis

Death of a Dream?

Once upon a time there was a shared dream of a community
Built on the strength of experience and a testament to society
Together in partnership with a bond of trust
The power embedded in both words and actions a must

Things to do every day made such a wonderful start
Peer support of all kinds, activities and even some art
Great progress for many was made
Rot setting in when some were forbade

Actions of one spoiling the progress of many
People drifting away cos it's not worth a penny
Lights flicker and people bicker
Making the end come even quicker

The dream at an end but then we awaken
Realisation dawns that we're not really shaken
Trials and efforts haven't been wasted
The real dream has only been tasted

The hunger continues we broaden our horizons
Embracing other stigma like they're our cousins
More in common than we first thought
United as a team a new battle to be fought

Different but similar the name of our game
Peer support comes back in the frame
In all of its guises it can work like real magic
Helping us avoid outcomes so tragic

There is a moral to this strange tale
Of when something great is starting to fail
A dream may seem to die but it's not at an end
We never know what's around the next bend

Part 2: This is Us

Containing Chaos

The apex of success comes from within
Through trials and tribulations, never give in
Well thought out plans, attempts on the whim
Give it your best and you're destined to win

Persistently starting and stopping, trying and failing
Struggling, persevering, ascending and finally prevailing
Looking back, one word comes to mind – "dammit"
How the hell did I get to this summit?

Things in the past I cannot forget
Not to be jeter aux oubliettes
Lest they return to give us torment
Allowing us to dwell in unhelpful lament

To err is human, to forgive is divine
Look at those things so deep down in a mine
Examine and analyse but don't you dare dwell
Lest you wish to return to that hell

To find peace try to forgive past decisions
In so doing you create fantastic new visions
Reliably unpredictable with notions and emotions
Learn to be a yachtsman in the bipolar oceans

Pathways mapped out by the challenges we face
A forever journey we must always embrace
One day at a time, one foot in front of the other
The key – keep it simple and don't let it smother

Poetic Symbiosis

Forgiveness?

Wanting to feel as free as a bird
Through intoxication – the clue is in the word
Just poison in your system
A means of reality escapism.

Just one drink or pill or hit
An unknown destination maybe just a pit
Recovery and relapse siblings in this abyss
Leaving those closest in anything but bliss

We seek the adrenaline of the moment
And get nowt but disappointment
Yet with the depths to which we fall
We wonder why they never call

Living with unforgiving
Perhaps our greatest misgiving
So hard for them to forgive us
So we just make a fuss

They may never understand why
It was us that made them cry
So we must learn to be repentant
Before we can find contentment

There will be those who won't forgive
With that we have to learn to live
The new life is worth so much more
There is no need to knock their door

Part 2: This is Us

Sent to Coventry

Central city furthest from the coast
It's here that we've gained the most .
The three spires blitzed, cathedral destroyed in fire
It's in the elephant's castle we are destined to retire

One from the north and gravy stained tea
Farmhand from Somerset preferred the scrumpy
Doctored in Brighton, matured in Black Country
Many miles between but now we're in unity

New homes in the city once used for exile
During a conflict filled with punishment and guile
That was centuries ago, it's now a new age
Extending a hand of friendship on a new cultural stage

Unique and multicultural, diversity abounds
Accepting each other from mixed cities and towns
Society is tested but we continue to grow
Showing that wartime courage of decades ago

An unlikely haven in days of yore
No longer punishment you have to endure
Like Lady Godiva we stand for everything true
It's here we were smiled on in the city Sky Blue

Poetic Symbiosis

Mélangé dans L'unité

An engine of creative genius fuelled by two powerful cores
One ignites the flames the other stokes its cause
Generations apart yet there's common ground we share
Running the train of poetic justice on mere friendship and flare

Well-oiled machinery, a unit of intellectual finesse
Of ideas, emotions and uncharted prowess
An unlikely union of experiences and minds
One of nature's most remarkable finds

Mere minnows in the oceans of literature
Creating the most amazing and unified picture
Just a few written words and spoken in verse
Maybe at times it seems a bit terse

In a brotherhood of sorts with unlikely peers
Dealing at speed with those imaginary fears
Thrown together purely accident
Perhaps even by celestial alignment

There are greater things in heaven and earth
Human knowledge represents just a dearth
How it all happened, this matters not
We are just grateful for all we have got

Churning out crazy poems now and again
Doesn't cause anyone any great pain
Making some sense of the inexplicable
At contradiction and gibberish we are fully able

Union of minds when dealing with life's puzzles
To help understand we must lose our own muzzles
Problems shared perhaps in a group
Clears your head of all that strife – merci beaucoup

Part 2: This is Us

Therapy Unmasked

Group therapy can be like talking in code
With like-minded brethren, maybe a hidden abode
Making a safe environment so you can open up
Telling it true with the occasional hiccup

Sharing concerns with feedback from your peers
Speak with one mouth and listen with two ears
Volumes of experiences, some give a clue
Others no more than just déjà-vu

Sat at a crossroads in a Tharn silhouette
Any move a gamble like playing roulette
A solo singer or as part of a band
You need at least one other to lend you a hand

No more a nomad lost in a mist
Armed with a compass your arm to twist
Follow the arrow when it stops spinning
Change your own script, it's time to start winning

Two steps forward and one in reverse
This is normal and nothing perverse
Still moving forwards to yourself you atone
Please remember you're still not alone

Victory's hard fought and though it might hurt
To keep on winning you cannot just flirt
Ongoing support is a must and so vital
To be "In Recovery" is a well-earned honorary title

Poetic Symbiosis

Lapine Lore

Blind arrogance and ignorance have their consequences
Lessons must be learned to foster great wisdom
For or against, it's all about balances
Truth is essential, no decisions at random

Starting with only a vision of what we desire
Fear, hope and challenge add fuel to the fire
Courage and friendship the key to the bonds
Knowledge and teaching discourage vagabonds

Camaraderie not deception the best way of life
Preserving community from unwanted strife
Rewarding compassion with bravery and love
Tenacity and loyalty worn like a glove

Information and organisation of most value
These are the things that make social glue
Subjugation or hidden agenda counterproductive
Work with the opposites and try to forgive

Pursuit of freedom through sacrifice and stamina
Is it fuelled by us or Deus Ex Machina
Finality of the fight now it's all over
Then it can be just like living in clover

Time passes by and it's time to let go
It's all been recorded, new seeds to sow
Those happenings in days of yore
To be told for ever in Lapine Lore

Inspired by "Watership Down" by Richard Adams (Pbl Rex Collings 1972) and the Martin Rosen animated film (1978)

Part 2: This is Us

La Guerre Cérébrale

Equal in appearance but all are Jekyll and Hydes
The masks of normality covering our other sides
Rocking back and forth across the borderline
Are we normal are we sane we guess we'll know in time

These thoughts are all normal, then there are those that aren't
Behaviours become aberrant and control them we think we can't
Some we seem to be born with and others it seems that we learn
No matter what the cause is we fear that in hell we will burn

For those we are born with choice might have little effect
Whilst for those that we learn the impact is very direct
This dichotomy hardly defines us but helps to find a way forward
To focus on clear diagnosis, select a treatment and move onward

Choices and control are two completely different things
Since time began affecting both peasants and kings
Often the result of unbalanced actions and emotions
Medicines and other therapies are not the magic potions

In some situations medication seems the only option
To subdue behaviours that are viewed as extremes
The other end of the spectrum relies on communication
The mélange in between a lottery of seemingly lunatic schemes

Serving in this padded lonely cell grant me lucidity of my folie
Let me avoid being blasé and the jacket that hugs me
Allow not your demons and la bête noire abbatue
There's no fluency to this prescription so we bid you Salut.

An exorcism of the mania the tide goes to and fro
Yet in this cerebral maelstrom you'll learn more than you know
Like Sanskrit in the caves the message we must decipher
The only thing that matters now is are we quitters or fighters

Poetic Symbiosis

Will Power or Willpower?

They said Will Power would help me
Who is he and where does he live?
To so many questions the answers he could give
What is the price on being set free?

I can't really answer, I don't know what to say
About the many dilemmas that face me every day
Spinning in a whirlpool life has completely lost control
Draining away like water funnelling down a plughole

Maybe it isn't a person but something from within
I understand the words but cannot find the meaning
Deep in frustration I'm bouncing off the ceiling
Further into the enigma, it's written in Mandarin

Is it just not giving in when things get a bit too tough
Or simply saying c'est la vie and that is good enough
Ready to throw the towel in and simply say I quit
Darkness turns into light to shine on that cesspit

Now it's clear that Will Power isn't a thing or being
It's what's inside us and what it is we're doing
Balancing between want and need is hardest fight
Willpower takes you either way, that's the biggest fright

The choice with this is in your hands so wisely you must act
Done with due diligence your dream can become a fact
Support in this is vital, the company we keep most crucial
Do not think this is all you need you're simply at the portal

The journey lasts forever but isn't set in stone
The final outcome ultimately will be yours alone
There always is a danger of reuniting with your pain
Staying on course is progress and needn't be a bane

Part 2: This is Us

So the secret of willpower is really plain to see
Just do the right things and you set yourself free
There is no illusion or magic, life is what it is
So shape it as you need it, be immune to toxicosis

Poetic Symbiosis

De-Termination

A journey with drink and drugs can be like riding on a carousel
Never ending circles on a galloping horse on the road to hell
The debt for seeking utopia unpayable but the ride is never free
The price you pay could be your life not just all your dignity

An arsenal of strategies needed to get your bottle or fix
Like a brand of street magic with a suitcase full of tricks
Lies, theft and prostitution the currency of the addict's purse
Your blood's gone bad, your skin is yellow it really is a curse

The urge to spend on drink and drugs so strong that it's hypnotic
Like the bells of Notre Dame the meaning can be mystic
You can hear a thousand voices but must listen to only one
Running the gauntlet fighting off the noises until the fight is won

Have the strength to leave that pack and carry on alone
It needn't be forever all alphas from cubs are grown
By giving out what you have learned you can take the lead
To develop a new battle plan with a better habit to feed

Life is a school that never closes, always a new class to take
If you stay on that carousel your short life will be a fake
If you don't change things and live forever by chance
Maybe you should simply invite the devil to dance

A new pack around you a new script and a new play
No silent harlequin in the wings and nothing at all to say
Through sheer determination the director is reborn
The guillotine of surrender is the light of a new dawn

Part 2: This is Us

E Pluribus Unum?

Society's dregs at the bottom of the barrel without a voice
In need of an advocate because we were given no choice
A system full of corruption and failures a real vol-de-mort
This evil of self-interest ultimately the truth will distort

Is it just a dream to have equal support and rights
Or betrayal of the Magna Carta that makes us see the light
Politics and statistics are all that seem to matter
Imposed glass ceilings the things that we must shatter

Should the advocate come from above or from below
It matters not but someone must pick up the gauntlet
"To speech not arms" the instrument we must bestow
That could be an armoured glove, words or a bullet

Strong argument by one on behalf of the masses
Society should be all together not divided by classes
Equality from the same core maleficence from the few
Listening more than talking the game starts anew

Co-existence should benefit all in equal measure
Not a reason for the few to bury some treasure
Better to live in harmony than to die in conflict
Be remembered for trying to get the right verdict

Poetic Symbiosis

Final Dilemma

Would I call it quits if I was to live for just one more day
All that good work undone and back into the fray
Those years of sobriety victories against the hordes
In my last hours should I change course

Liquid courage was once my only true friend
Mon Ami, am I destined to be with you at the end
This chasm of questions this lingering doubt
All I have achieved will finally mean nowt

At this final place in la guerre cérébrale
This battle's prize is neither heaven nor hell
Today is my last so could I, would I, should I
Take that last drink as carpe diem, my coup de grâce

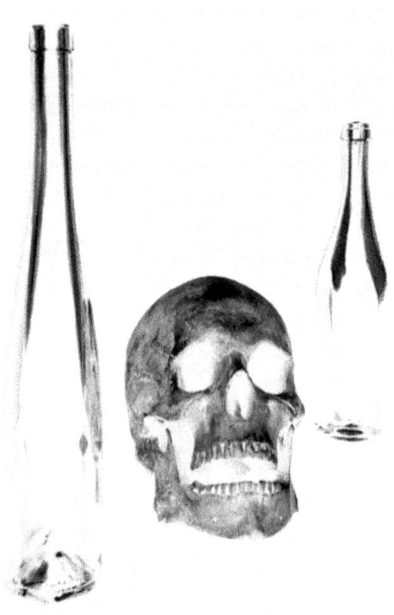

Part 2: This is Us

Labelling Faux Pas

Is a label just something on a packet nestled outside?
That sets out to tell us what it has inside
Or could there more invisible to the eye
Those hidden ingredients to find them we pry

Labels on people they tell us much less
So many things that we don't want to confess
The label an umbrella to treat them as an alien race
Such selectivity is quite simply a total disgrace

Are we blind when we use words instead of sight?
Intellect not terminology decides what is wrong or right
Names for this and that but what's in a name
The structure of labels and lyrics is a whole new game

So often the negative denying their best
In that way they are all seen to be only a pest
Ignoring the positive denies their humanity
Stripping them all of most of their dignity

Underneath that label there is so much more
All are human beings and should be treated as such
Great characteristics can be found to be sure
In thoroughness and honesty to these we must clutch

How do we decipher the hieroglyphics of our uncertainty?
The silence of embarrassment can lead to melancholy
Falseness and fakery arise when we don't understand
How we can co-exist peacefully in this wonderful land

Poetic Symbiosis

Constructive Distraction

Distraction takes your mind off what it is you are doing
Coming and going it surfs and crashes the walls of your mind
Shifting focus through visual illusions and words that are dancing
Trying to use that sextant of focus to realign and stop being blind

As a phantom trident its prongs each have a separate end
Following the wrong one will drive you round the bend
The first will prevent you completing the task in hand
The second keeps prodding most savagely, an unforgiving brand

The third distracts in a most constructive guise
The mask it produces freeing the hands and mind
In synchronicity we see things through new eyes
Our original mission now coming to a swift end

This culmination the reward of a cerebral rift
Not a trophy but an internal pride
For not having to avoid, evade or hide
Perversely distraction was my greatest gift

Part 2: This is Us

Perfidious Faith

Faith is something we all need but comes with many precepts
From invisible deities at one extreme through to friends who are dear
Some are dominated by dogma and zealots with strange concepts
Maybe with devils, boggarts and spectres to fill us with fear

Faith can be blind or scripted in code with questions not allowed
Creating a cauldron of doubt from the fables that are told
It shifts our focus to what goes on within if we are bold
Yet any faith is as individual as a person lost in a crowd

It needs to be positive and never hubristic lest nemesis prevails
In other words do what is right with no desire to go off the rails
Maybe helped by external forces we can't get off the shelves
But most of all we must all have trust and faith in ourselves

Poetic Symbiosis

Liquiphrenic Conversation?

You promised you'd stay clean and sober
Again and again it's something I can never get over
You have no honour and deserve no sympathy
What can you do to change this impropriety

My darling, my head just screams "Foutre"
I've boarded a runaway train to nowhere
It just goes faster and faster and no way to stop
No-one is driving, I am off track and ready to drop

Waiting for an almighty crash my only friend is my vice
So I cling to Mon Ami like a new cub to his mother
That milk that should nurture is nothing but poison
That nourishment is just like beauty and the beast

Hanging on the cliff edge by one hand, time is going slow
Still hugging Mon Ami in the other, should I let him go
With that hand free I could reach out hoping to find help
Now I know I need to be saved only from myself

My darling I do believe you are finally at your nadir
I could simply let you go or reach out and pull you near
If I let go it must be forever with no turning back
If I reach out things must change, let's start it with a chat

To help, so little that I can do, mostly it's down to you
You need to change, shed that outer skin and be laid bare
Then create a new skin, new chance and a new life
Not quite a snake in ecdysis because you have changed inside

Part 2: This is Us

Guerrilla Warfare

"Veni, vidi, vici" their arrogant and defiant boast
Napoleon Complex just their Achilles heal
Like their hero they will meet their Waterloo
Bellicose to the end against impossible odds

Like the walls of Jericho their world will tumble down
Still they laugh like Batman's Joker on the riven streets
Unlike a Mexican Standoff carnage is almost inevitable
Time for citizens to unite against this anarchic lunacy

The inmates have overrun the asylum the doors are unlocked
An open barrage of barricades opposing forces at an impasse
This urban carnival free to those who embrace the clown
Their arch-nemesis now applying the tactics of war

Those bastard politicians their ethos holds us down
Like street militia an organised fighting unit is formed
Urban Gorillas beating their chests in a concrete jungle
Performing a Maori haka they go back to tribal war

Time has gone by and a truce is called, it's time to talk
At the table the cards are drawn, the whisky on the table
Time to show the hands and the winner takes it all
Anarchy the dead man's hand, Wellington's royal flush calls

Poetic Symbiosis

Multimasking

In frenzied moments of chaotic behaviour are we wearing a mask?
Or is it every day we wear a different one depending on our task?
Is life a menagerie wanting us to be a different animal each day?
Perhaps simply being ourselves should be the only true way

Many grease-painted mute harlequins are lurking in the wings
Dressed in charming sparkling costumes, scowling or with grins
Their silence is subtle yet so powerful we need to take control
Ringmaster don the top hat, pick up the cane, it's time to rock and roll

The resulting burlesque stuns the crowd into wild applause
Our greatest show sets the stage on fire, literally of course
Laughter turns to fear, their rapturous awe to infernal panic
The freaks on stage feel normal it's the audience that are comic

Now the roles are reversed, the cast are in the credits
The audience's five star performance worthy of our merit
Children in the crowd in trauma, tearfully baptised in anxiety
Fearing murder someone picks up another mask – responsibility

Time to bring this to an end, a final costume change
Today I have been many souls most of them are strange
This episode is over, it seemed so real, I know that I am hurting
My mind a mask of many faces, it's time to close the curtain

Part 2: This is Us

Mechanically Human

People embodied in skin and bones
With mortal function and emotional tones.
Fibres and pigments that have invisible transparency,
A skeletal foundation forming humanity

Machines made of metals and materials no essence of connection,
Just programmed with artificial intelligence a robotic rebellion
The curse of being human is the ability to feel
Making us in awe at the wonders all around us

Not just in colours of gold red white and teal
Or objects that simply follow procedure
Mort mais vivant not a corpse of cogs bolts and wheels
What colour is its blood what pains do they feel

Emancipation in the art of surviving without a kill switch
A decision of our own an original not a Xerox
Produced by a machine solitary and unknown
Cloning on repeat on an assembly line

Humans can behave like that
Just like that inanimate machine
Doing the same stupid things in routine
As if we are preconditioned to behave in a loop

Our DNA is only a rough blueprint
Born with mortality and the right to be wrong
It's determined by experience and choices
Remember you are human and not a machine

Poetic Symbiosis

Crisis of a Human Rose

The walls are closing in, the desperate urges and rattling sound
Getting louder and louder and hologram visions take control
I'm joining the Suicide Squad, will soon be reverse six feet tall
But do I really want to end it, I'll give the Crisis Team a call

Minutes on the phone, in the waiting room and queue
They're a crisis in a crisis for all the good they'll do
Have a cup of tea they say a warm bath and your meds
They ignore the fact that I use spring showered grass for my bed

Apparently it's good to talk about what sways in your mind
But take this pill and sleep, why thank you you're so kind
To the bottom of the heap I go, shuffled like a standard deck
The crisis team are there for you, are they fucking heck

Ever needed an ear to hear you or someone to hold your hand
They just pass the buck you know yet they're meant to understand
Now the crisis crew aren't all useless – well actually they are
No better than high paid drug dealers that drive a company car

I've gone a thousand rounds and the soundtracks on repeat
They'll be better off without you, give in to your defeat
Popping pills like candy whilst waiting for the crisis dealer
If they're not here soon I'll go visit the old grim reaper

Bloodied arms, an empty bottle, now it's getting dark and I'm all alone
Finally they've turned up full of words and a packet of Zopiclone
No signs of help or support, I'm just a burden on their shift
Maybe I'm a lucky one who gets nothing out of this

Part 2: This is Us

All alone again in the spider's web, not sure if I'll pull through
These sounds are different but so loud I just want to say adieu
So would you call the Crisis Team to prevent surrender and death?
To be honest I wouldn't, I'd just accept sadly that I've done my best

Poetic Symbiosis

Not Like That

Remembering things that we did long ago
Those terrible things that we cannot let go
So many things we would rather forget
It's not like that anymore

We always asked why we did what we did
Couldn't give an answer so just went and hid
Doing more stupid things and not knowing why
It's not like that anymore

So many years with getting things wrong
Made us think that we didn't belong
With friends, family or the human race
It's not like that anymore

So many attempts to turn things around
So many times going back underground
Why we couldn't change we'll never know
It's not like that anymore

The penny finally drops for reasons unknown
Finding new friends and no longer alone
One hell of a struggle in those early days
It's not like that anymore

Days, weeks, months and years go by
Now having fun, how time does fly
Getting better slowly seems such a chore
It's not like that anymore

Finding a new life with everything bettered
At long last completely unfettered
Still not sure how anything changed
It's not like that anymore

Part 2: This is Us

Knowing now we will never know how
Just let it all go and a new life you will plough
So much better that all you need to say is
It's not like that anymore

Poetic Symbiosis

Doolally in Deolali

Doolally tapped in this hot Asian sun
Like that concert party all having fun
At home or abroad a regime of boredom
In limbo of anticipation the march of Mongol Hun

Native and foreign alike just biding their time
In suspended animation till called to attention
Stood in a parade line in costumes so fine
Ready to put on a hell of a show ... say the word and it's a go

An audience as crazy as the performers themselves
Driven totally doolally from being assigned jankers
"SHUT UP" the only command they obey
A commission of the sergeant stripes proudly on display

With a whispering in the grass and beds of bamboo
Like Hitler's advance into Russia it's completely cuckoo
The brothers in arms born in jungle loyalty
An empire of great size for an island so small but fond of tea

A fine pair of shoulders to carry a nation
Crazed in conflict a legal murder of audio-hallucinations
Lewd thoughts in a basha completely of men
"It aint half hot mum" we say over and over again

La-di-da ivories and songs in English and Urdu
The Home Guard of old, glory to the many on sacrifice of the few
Jaldi the monsoon madness creeps in to officers of all class
Lovely boys with their artistry vocal and visual ... a unique warlike
tact

Part 2: This is Us

Through the history of Britain and her greatness and Commonwealth
Size doesn't matter it's the faith and fight you carry inside yourself
The Land of Hope and Glory and proudly Who Dares Wins
Salute the Jack and stand united we're flying without wings

"Don't let the bastards grind you down" the great British spirit
Two world wars and a World Cup these three lions roar not quit
Monarchs of old King George III they called him mad
But is being completely doolally really all that bad

Mental, folie or crazy these terms are only words
Though their impact injects a venom for better or for worse
It won't be forever this doolally state you can leave behind
Windsor Davies said it best "Oh dear how sad never mind"

(Scripted with a nod to all military veterans and British television humour of the 1970s)

Poetic Symbiosis

La Bête Noire

Winston Churchill called it his black dog
To a drunk it's that bottle of grog
To a junkie a fix instead of a feast
To others maybe multiple beasts

Whatever it is it wears you right down
Causing much more than simply a frown
Tearing apart much worse than a broken heart
Leaving you feeling ready for that mortuary cart

For every yin there is a mandatory yang
When in darkness the obvious solution is light
Balancing opposites prevents that loud bang
Allowing you to live life without too many a fright

Complementary balances switching back and forth
Creating sustainability with distractions each way
Like travelling east to west with dips south and north
Still achieving the goal sometimes to your own dismay

That black beast not always the dominant force
Brief encounters create essential breaks from the task
Letting in fresh thinking like changing your horse
Getting there quickly despite flip-flopping your mask

Getting the balance right is a bit of an art
Not simply under your conscious control
Recognising its triggers makes a good start
If they are your choices you can earn parole

When they are spontaneous you may need some help
They may not be choices but come from within
Speak to someone who understands don't just yelp
They can give good guidance so you can win

Part 2: This is Us

Then there is always L'Ange Blanc although he's barking mad
The pleasure he brings counters all that's dark and bad
The light that he shines gives us inspiration
To generate rapidly another new creation

Poetic Symbiosis

An Eternal Labyrinth II

People living with mental health issues are called patients
Whilst those living with addiction are just called pathetic
The former seen as ill and the latter just guilty of abrogation
Two sides of the same coin no-one is immune when they flip it

Navvy, doctor or high court judge all are fair game to the curses
Left unmanaged with either the end game is simply in hearses
Instant suicide or a slow decay as bodily systems shut down
Death can take different turns but all lead to a white gown

The addict can have an advantage the cause of their chaos quite clear
Choices can be made to control things but maybe not easy to make
The paranoid schizophrenic can do little in a life that is filled with fear
Drugs powerful tools for the patient but an addict's friend, no mistake

Again both sides of the coin so why should we make any distinctions
The human mind a complex machine with millions of interconnections
The mechanisms of the malfunctions rarely understood and deciphered
This means that those with these issues feel as if they are buggered

They can be of help to each other and support groups are manifold
Some are condition specific whilst others might be open to all
Sharing in group can be tough but they become increasingly bold
In many different forms but so helpful in preventing that final fall

Part 2: This is Us

The Addiction Clover

Trapped in tunnel vision an isolated charge
Of personal gain and desire the unknowing thrill
The reward of the hunt and then the sweetest kill
Four points of the compass and sides of life's square
To catch that rabbit with a continuous streak

That's ultimately living without care
Be it that win on the one armed bandit
Or scoring that liquid you want
Even that bag of small crystals
A risk in a dangerous game silly cunt

Alcohol Gambling and Narcotics too
These are the ones who win
Every time you spin the wheel
Haul your pint and shot
Or cook up that metal pin

Three out of four leaves us dead
Or bankrupt and broken
Fourth is the counter a substitute ready to be awoken
It's never easy to break the habit or circles of safety
We need to lead and not be led

Every win is shadowed with loss
Brain cells friends and family you don't give a toss
We came to trust our old behaviours
But we need to be addicted to living
Not persistently substance dependent

Poetic Symbiosis

The A to Z of Mental Health and Addiction

A is for addiction and anxiety
B is for borderline and bipolar
C is for crisis and chaos
D is for depression and drugs
E is for emotional and empty
F is for family and friends
G is for grog and grief
H is for heroin and homeless
I is for illness and intrigue
J is for Jack Daniels and Jameson's
K is for kilo and ketamine
L is for LSD and loss
M is for marijuana and meds
N is for no hope and nothing
O is for opportunity and oh fuck it
P is for prison and pain
Q is for quantity and queues
R is for rattling and robbery
S is for scoring and shaking
T is for theft and triggers
U is for using and unstable
V is for vodka and veins
W is for withdrawals and wasted
X is for X-rated and Xanax
Y is for you and Yaba
Z is for Zoly and Zopiclone

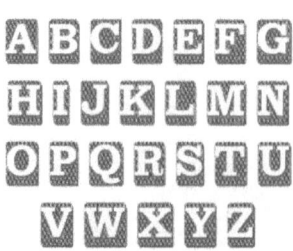

Part 2: This is Us

The Z to A of Recovery

A is for acceptance and action
B is for bravery and brethren
C is for commitment and care
D is for determination and doggedness
E is for effort and enterprise
F is for fantastic and fun
G is for great and growth
H is for health and happiness
I is for initiative and independence
J is for justice and just for today
K is for karma and keep going
L is for life and love
M is for magic and momentum
N is for now and never again
O is for optimism and openness
P is for peaceful and persistence
Q is for quiet and quality of life
R is for right and regular
S is for safe and success
T is for taste and truth
U is for utmost and unveil
V is for valiant and victory
W is for wise and willing
X is for xenophile and X-ray vision
Y is for yes and yippee
Z is for zest and zebra crossing

Poetic Symbiosis

Trigger Happy

I'm walking along this road, I don't know where it leads
Like that great oak tree I pass, life has planted seeds
Fear and doubts have taken root and can grow at any time
These smells of history can cause repeat of my former crime

The sound of silence may be a comfort or a torment
When dates stick in my mind and lead me to lament
They hurt the same today, enough to make me cry
Wild actions of untamed anger, I always wonder why

Like the walking dead, I zombie soulless without speech
Coz there's been words that nearly killed me and left me on the beach
I keep my eyes closed trying to avoid so many familiar places
I'm not the one who led us here, you scarred me with your faces

The way you move and stand, the posture you have set
I just want to run and hide, I wish we'd never met
Cold dark and numb, everything is out to get me
Trauma and its members will force me into slavery

Mountain rivers and roads, I find there's no escape
I'm triggered by the bloody lot, I must accept this fate
I can't go on anymore the past always seems to win
If only I could understand a new life I could begin

My body, my heart and brain are scarred, all of them together
There's no light at the end, the tunnel's closed and stained
Trigger's not just a horse's name but in the mind forever
All hidden and unknown but they have you fully trained

Part 2: This is Us

Sobriety Junktion

Picture a dry drunk and a junkie no longer trainspotting
This scientific art of recovery is remembering not forgetting
Is it simply a recipe or a formula that we must follow?
Start by saying there is hope and we will reach tomorrow

The former ways of conduct and that behaviour spasm
Are still there in the background like lava in the chasm
The art of being sober it sounds so easy to simply act it out
After a day or a year there will always be that lingering doubt

Life will always test us and break us like a fragile antique
Strength in your ability to change found in a rare boutique
Daily routines and positive influence aren't all that you need
You've grown to amazing heights by applying haste not just speed

The simplicity of A B C the plotted path with edges straight
Like a spew of vomit that spreads deliriously across the plate
Choices, changes and control the new ways of the spring dove
Though be pre-warned that those old habits still fit like a glove

The grog, powders, pills and pin forever our perfect friends
They made good that vow to destroy our common sense
Recovery an art of science learned from a book and debated in class
Professor Life the finest teacher but even he will bite you in the ass

Poetic Symbiosis

Cockney Intro

After the emotional journey we have both experienced revisiting chaotic periods of our lives, we mutually agreed to continue writing along our themes of addiction and mental health, but in a more light-hearted way. The following effort is an example of how we can use free-running, aberrant, thinking as a form of recovery from the hard-hitting process we had been through.

We hope you have as much fun reading this as we had when writing it!

A Cockney on the Cobbles

Allo me ole china, fancy a rabbit. Guess wot I wuz nicked by the Bill the aver day, accused me of robbin a jam – wot a load of Brad. We wuz just avin a butchers on the way to get a ruby. The ole trouble went barmy but I told her to keep her Barnet on and that led to a full blown bull. Anyway we went dahn the rub to elp clear me napper and got a good few down me Gregory and ended up very Brahms. Some Berk opened is norf so I gave im a smack in the boat. Er skin was there on the dog bein a pain in the Khyber so I grabbed er by the Bristols and it went even more Pete when she kneed me in the cobblers. Then I was all on me Jack out in the taters wivaht a weasel. Anyway, there wuz I staggerin dahn the frog when plod shows up again. Same two rozzers and I reckon one of them was jinja so I told im so and I'd see im up the apples. The two Hamptons took me off me plates and slammed me in the floweries for the night wivart me daisies, belt and bees. Next mownin it was before the Richard of a beak and got fined a bag. That was me night aht!

Poetic Symbiosis

Epilogue

Poetic Symbiosis was written between late 2019 and early 2020, with the publication process beginning just as the coronavirus pandemic hit the UK. The subsequent lockdown really sharpened our minds since we were no longer able to have our regular Wednesday afternoon writing sessions. Furthermore, our regular support group meetings also went out of the window. We both live alone and have found the use of modern technology so valuable in staying sane, whatever that is! Simple phone calls are great, but the advantages provided by video calls and conferences cannot be underestimated in these difficult times. They can be life-savers and, if you have unlimited data on your broadband, they can cost absolutely nothing!

To prove the point, we co-wrote the following poem remotely, using voice and video calls on the phone network and WhatsApp, supported by email. OK, it has been a different way of working but we have managed to maintain the spirit of banter and collaboration whilst in isolation.

QED

Matt and The Doc, April 2020

Poetic Symbiosis

Isolate and Collaborate: Antithesis?

The world in social isolation, sanity can drift
Alone in remote solitary a nightmare or a gift
Talk and talk some more the message we encourage
On the phone or with a text, clutching try to salvage

Government says work from home if you can
Livelihoods are frozen, jobs, schools aren't to plan
Panic buying and people crying – population lost
Self-protect and hide away but at what cost?

Limits on our outings, curfews hard in place
Rules and regulations "do not touch your face"
Will this last forever or just a month or two?
How long till we can see each other I don't know, do you?

The distance is a struggle, right?
In achieving that which we must
Thursday at eight we united that night
Trajectory's like a roller coaster, beware of the dust

Going stir because the kids are bored
No entertainment reach for the grog, things are bad
Or break the lockdown, be a rebel what have you to lose?
Just your life apparently, according to the news

Some fought for freedom in a world war
Now our heroes use medicines not guns
Though these restrictions cause rest and now I'm unsure
Maybe if we lock the cage "coronavirus will do one"

Collaborating on our words whilst distancing afar
The process shot to shit "where's that whisky jar?"
Deep down we all have fear, no-one saw this coming
One day we'll beat this, I hope that day is coming this morning

Epilogue

Isolation and collaboration seem mutually exclusive
Not at all dear friends we can still be all-inclusive
No we are not talking about some fake codology
The secret clearly lies in our modern technology

Snail-mail might be one way of staying in touch
Too slow you cry I need a response right now
Turn to technology and use this as a crutch
Providing powerful tools, you need to learn how

Not quite the same as talking face to face
In one-to-one meetings or as part of a group
Better than nothing, up your sleeve it's an ace
Maintaining your senses to your sanity recoup

Your phone, tablet, laptop or personal computer
Using Skype, WhatsApp, Zoom or whatever
You can see all those faces that give so many clues
Lots of support in your home whilst paying no dues

Poetic Symbiosis

www.ingramcontent.com/pod-product-compliance
Lightning Source LLC
Chambersburg PA
CBHW071314040426
42444CB00009B/2014